FASCINATING
HORSES

FASCINATING
HORSES

Tomáš Míček

REBO PRODUCTIONS

All the photographs in this book were taken on Canon cameras.

Original title: Faszinierende Pferde

Cover design: Ton Wienbelt, The Hague, The Netherlands
Translation: Stephen Challacombe
Editing: Elke Doelman
Production: TextCase, Groningen, The Netherlands
Typesetting: Hof&Land Typografie, Maarssen, The Netherlands

ISBN 1 84053 0375

Contents

Introduction

The natural habitat for a horse are the wide open savannah and open steppes. It needs air and light, wind and sun, snow and rain, the warmth of the day and the chill of the night, the difference between summer and winter. It feels at home in a herd, protected by the stallion and led by the most important mare.
The horse is naturally a slow, deliberate eater but it also has natural flight instincts. It has to try to escape its enemies by tremendous galloping strides.
Horses race each other to see which is fastest. They will travel far in search of fresh pastures.
In the natural conditions of the steppes, horses remain constantly on the move. Movement is the most important characteristic of a horse.
Movement provides escape from danger, so movement means life.
The leading photographer Tomás Mícek is extraordinarily interested in this natural movement and has captured the motion of outstanding breeds of horse with his camera.
The secret of these photographs is the natural, and unforced demeanour of the subjects, for he prefers to photograph horses that are free to roam. Posed photographs or harnessed horses do not appeal to him. Of course a certain amount of direction is required to achieve some of the images.
Mícek observes, waits and captures the stirring, remarkable, and exciting moment. The vitality, dash, and energy of these animals is a magnificent wonder to him, because he revels in the animation and the rhythm of their movements.
Mícek has tremendous enthusiasm for photographing horses and he does so with heart and soul. It is not just the bold movements that he seeks to capture, but also the variations and subtle nuance of expression of their eyes, ears and muzzles.
His photographs convey the temperament and personality of the animals. His successful method requires patience without losing sight of animation and vitality.
The result is photographs of "wild" horses, and of horses with a great degree of freedom.
Wherever possible in his travels throughout Europe, he tries to photograph horses in surroundings that are as natural as

possible. With great sensitivity and tremendous professionalism, he has selected a remarkable collection from a considerable volume of superb photographs to create this photo-essay as his tribute to ten breeds of horse which are descendants from the noblest bloodlines.
The elegant, lithe, and pure-blood Arabs were photographed in the sea on the shores of the Atlantic Ocean and also in the south of France, Hesse in Germany, and Upper Austria.
The strong, sturdy horses of the Camargue were photographed in their own surroundings in the Rhône delta. A herd of Thoroughbreds at a stud in southern Moravia gallop straight at the viewer.
The puissant images of Friesian horses caught on film in North Rhine-Westphalia remind one of the extremely powerful horses of times past. Captivating photographs of Welsh Cobs were taken in Austria and Mícek's pictures of attractive Lipizzaner stallions, which have the quality of paintings, were created in Austria and Lipica in Slovenia.
The photographs of powerful Fjord stallions playfully duelling with each other come from Bavaria and the superb portrait, movement, and winter studies of high-spirited Haflingers are from across the border in Tyrol.
A herd of hardy Icelandic ponies was also photographed in the snow.
Tomás Mícek's first love though is the elegant Andalusian horse. This favourite, lovely creature has been set against the wild flower meadows and beaches of Andalusia. His remarkable photographs capture the intelligence and equable nature of this Spanish breed.

This richly illustrated book displays the magnificence and character of noble horses in photographs that are a feast for the eye for one and all, whether or not they are horse lovers

Arabian horses along the ocean shores

According to legend, Poseidon created the horse by thrusting his trident out of the sea. Consequently there is a close relationship in Greek mythology between the horse and water. The following photographs recall Poseidon, god of the sea and shore. They show pure-blooded Arab mares galloping in the Atlantic Ocean in the Bay of Biscay and charging ashore from the sea. The lithe, graceful movements of these elegant creatures contrasts with the unbridled force of the untamed Atlantic Ocean with its thundering breakers, stormy waves, and foaming surf.

A true Arab chestnut mare in the ocean's surf.

In the thundering breakers of the Atlantic Ocean

According to legend, the horse as created from the waves of the sea

The marsh horses of the Camargue

The horses of the Camargue live in the morasses of the Rhône delta. This strong breed of large horses is renowned for its instinctive sure footing on swampy and marshy ground. With the help of ancient remains that have been found, the origins of this breed have been dated to the Quaternary geological era. When the Moors invaded Southern France in 730, it is probable that some Arab and Barb blood was introduced but the difficult living conditions of these horses has meant that any incursions by stallions of other breeds will have been short-lived. The only influences still recognisable are traces of eastern bloodlines, in particular the Barb.

The demands on the horses of the legendary cattle herders of the Camargue, who round up the black, nimble bulls, have always been high. At present there are about 1,000 true, pedigree Camargue horses in the entire world. Their goatee beard is a sign of breed purity – long, coarse hairs run from beneath the chin to the lower lip.

Even when the horses are born dark-coloured, their coat become snow white as they get older.

Camargue horses enjoy water and are able to graze on tender shoots of reeds under water with their nostrils closed.

They usually spend the entire year on the reed beds and salt flats. With their agile and strong legs with broad hooves, they are ideally adapted to their surroundings.

The photographs taken in the Camargue give a characteristic impression of these strong, tireless, and insatiable horses.

Horses of the Camargue gallop through the shallow waters of the marshland

Heads raised, nostrils flared, manes streaming – the horses of the Camargue charge through shallow water.

"All that freedom and to roam with them; I would give anything to be a horse."

Count Von Odiel

Gelded riding horses thunder across the reed-beds of the Camargue

Andalusian horses – Spanish nobles

The home of the Andalusian horse is in the south-west of the Iberian peninsula. Horses have been bred here for many centuries. Andalusia is the part of Spain that was conquered by the Moors in the eighth century. During the Moorish rule, blood-lines from Berber horses (present day Barb) were favourably introduced to the native Spanish horses.
Other blood was introduced from the heavy horses of the Goths who ruled the area for about one hundred years. The result was the Andalusian horse, which has a pedigree stretching back as the "Pura Raza Espanola" which is one of the longest enduring in the world. These elegant horses were favourites for parades because of their natural high leg action. The Andalusian lifts its foreleg almost to chest height and turns its hoof outwards as it lands. During the annual festival in Seville, riders like to show off their horse's striking gait as a side-show to the magnificent costumes of the bullfighters and estate owners. But the proverbial elegance of these horses should never be allowed to overshadow the fact that they are also outstanding for their strength and docile nature. Wonderful photographs were taken in Andalusia of superb stallions, and mares with their foals, against a background of meadows filled with abundant wild flowers. The oriental grey colouring is superbly set off against brightly-coloured spring flowers and clear azure skies. The flowing manes of wavy hair and metallic sheen of the coats of Andalusians serve to emphasize their grace.
The viewer is fascinated by the litheness of these noble Spaniards. It is as if they dance.

Andalusian stallion in a meadow copiously filled with wild spring flowers

Mastil the Stallion lifts his slender foreleg. This striking gait has made the Andalusian a coveted parade horse.

The black stallion Tribuno stretches his head and shoulders forwards. He has detected a scent – perhaps it is that of his rival Quilate.

Tenderly, this mare nuzzles her foal

Expressive portrait of the stallion Valido

The waves in the sand of the dunes are echoed in the muscular form of the stallion.

"The boy dreamed of the white stallion, until the day that he grasped him by the mane."

Antonio Machado

While grazing, Vasallo the stallion has detected an interesting scent amid all the spring flowers.

Full gallop – the Thoroughbred in motion

The Thoroughbred – a breed that most people solely associate with speed and performance – owes its existence to the English obsession with horse-racing and betting. The first studbook for horses was produced in 1793, and every Thoroughbred since shares its bloodlines with those original progenitors in an unbroken line across more than thirty generations. The three original bloodlines came from Beyerley Turk, Darley Arabian, and Godolphin Barb that were imported into Britain around 1700. These horses are the forefathers of about eighty per cent of all the full-blooded horses in the world.

Beyerley Turk, the oldest of the three, was a Turkish stallion that the British officer Beyerley took as spoils of war during the siege of Vienna in 1683.

Darley Arabian, the only one of the three from Arabia, appealed because of his perfect beauty. This stallion came into the possession of the British Consul Thomas Darley in 1704, who established one of the principal bloodlines of the English Thoroughbred.

Godolphin Barb came from Tangiers and was a gift from the ruler of Morocco to the French court of Louis XV. Because the king considered the horse to be so ugly – the Barb stallion had an extremely thick neck, pig-like ears, and rounded hindquarters – the horse was either given away or sold. An English breeder called Cooke found the horse pulling a water cart in Paris and took him home with him to England. The son, Lath, was the most famous racehorse of his age, and his father became one of the forefathers of Thoroughbred breeding. The photographs show Thoroughbreds in the most appropriate way, at full gallop. Let the colts gallop straight at you in a heaving mass of horse flesh. The graceful, strong and sinewy, noble Thoroughbreds have powerful, imposing hooves. The pictures were taken in southern Moravia.

Two colts thunder across Moravian turf.

"The great mass of such noble animals approaches at full gallop."

Johann Wolfgang von Goethe

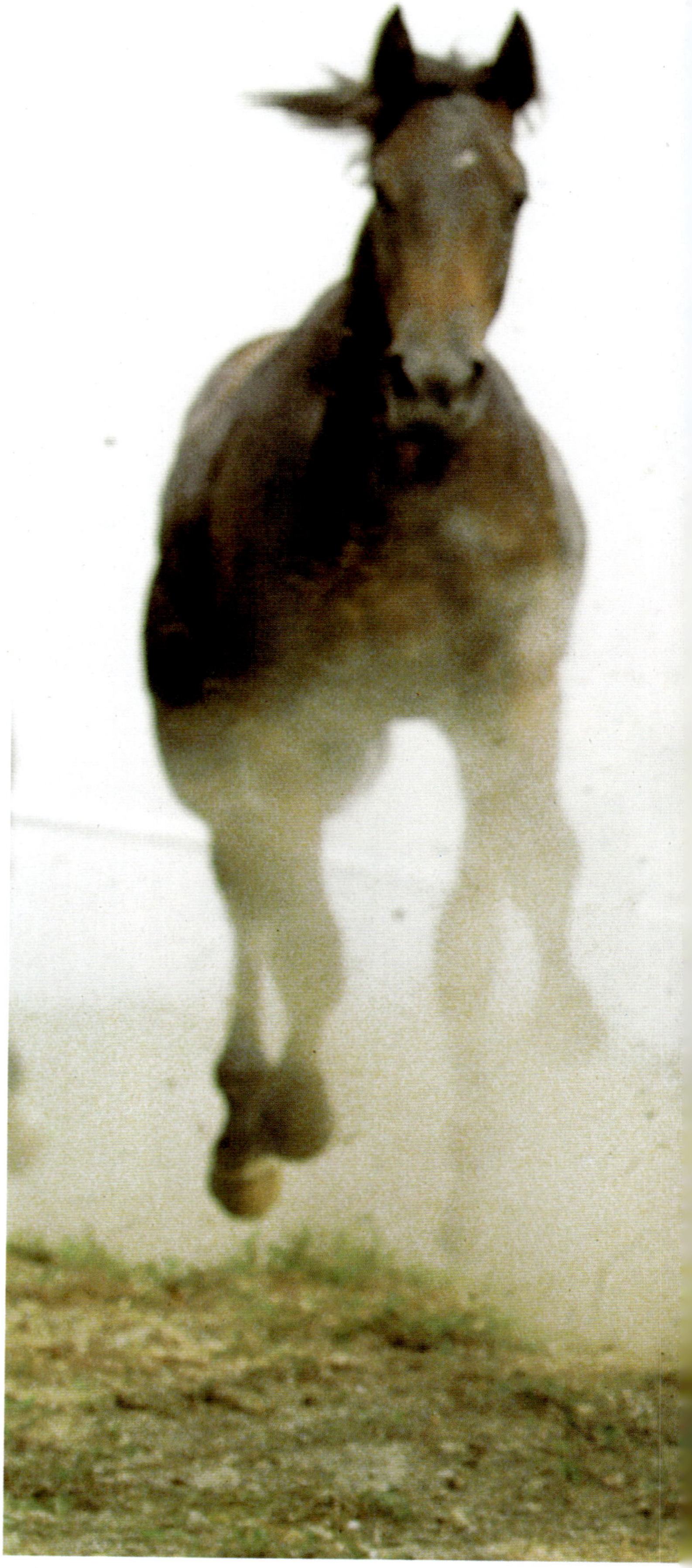

Could these be descendants of Pegasus, the winged horse?

"A horse gallops with his lungs, keeps going with his heart, and wins through his character."

Frederico Tesio

The pure-blood Arab – creature of the southern wind

Lovers of horses probably know the legend about the creation of the horse according to those nomads of the deserts of Arabia, the Bedouin. They says that God breathed a southerly wind from which the horse was created.
The pure-blood Arabs certainly originate from the desert region, where they were used a steeds. The nomads are considered to have been the original breeders of the Arab horse.
Mohammed is deemed to have given them the horse to keep them company in their tent with the admonition that the breed must remain pure.
The Bedouin only bred horses with a perfect pedigree, regardless of whether the animals were beautiful or fast. However, only the best and strongest horses could survive the forced treks that lasted for days, and these horses provided the breeding stock.
Consequently the characteristics of the breed, such as speed, stamina, strength, and courage, together with the ability to perform well until quite old, have been retained. The way in which an Arab gallops with his head held high has gained them the nickname of "drinker of the air." Large, expressive eyes and a concave profile are typical of a pure-bred Arab.
This sensitive, and inquisitive mount calls for understanding riders who will appreciate his intelligence and dignity. The lithe and graceful movements of these horses excites the eye.
The photographs, that were taken in the south of France, Hesse, and Upper Austria, not only wonderfully convey the elegance and grace of these horses, but also reveal their sensitive nature.

Puissant elegance of an Arab stallion with mane and tail streaming, and not one hoof touching the ground.

Elegance, grace, and nobility are united in the movements of a pure-bred Arab stallion

Left: the foal puckers his lips and learns to whicker.
Above: the mare trots delicately through dandelions while the foal gamely gallops beside her.

Stallion and mare bill and coo before mating.

Friesian horses – the heavy superhorse

The light-footed coldblood Friesian breed originates from the north-east of the Netherlands.

The stallions and geldings are high-spirited but well-behaved. Their most obvious feature is the extensive feather over the pastern. Despite their great strength and stamina, the gentle-nature of these "black pearls", as they are often called, is impressive.

The cattle-breeders of the Friesian tribes probably began breeding fairly small to medium-sized black horses with a high leg-action from as early as 12 BC, to pull their wagons.

In the Middle Ages, these horses were favoured as war horses. The Franks, who converted the Friesians to Christianity, introduced new blood to the breed and later the Andalusian horse and eastern stallions changed their appearance and created a lighter, more manoeuvrable horse. These horses became the ceremonial horses of the European monarchies. Today, the tremendous draught ability and speed of these imposing horses catch the eye.

The photographs, which were taken in North Rhine-Westphalia, conjure up notions of the powerful horses of mythology on which the gods thundered across the heavens. They ruled the world from the backs of such gleaming horses. Perhaps, instead, you imagine the Friesian as an armoured steed bearing a knight into battle, charging the enemy at a mighty gallop.

The superb photographs capture the exceptional dynamism and overwhelming power and beauty of these geldings.

The high-spirited movement of these black stallions are exceptional for their powerful dynamism.

"The long manes fell across their backs like wigs. They had mighty hooves that were equally festooned with bundles of hair, which flowed like plumes when they galloped."

Pablo Neruda

Delightful Welsh Cobs

The genealogists cannot agree about the origins of these horses. The question is whether they are derived from the native Welsh ponies, Yorkshire Coach Horses, Arabs, Thoroughbreds, and Hackneys, or from the Welsh Mountain Pony, and local cart horses. In either event, the Welsh Cob has changed little in appearance since about 1800. Paintings of this era depict the strong legs, arched back, and noble head that are still typical of the breed.

These are predominantly cross-country horses with strong bones, or good-natured hacks sturdy enough for adults, with an ability to jump well, inherited from cross-breeding with large part-bred horses.

A noble disposition and modesty, animatedly friendly, and proverbial courage are characteristics of these horses, which have the tremendous advantage of being suitable for many purposes – family pony or top-level competition – without needing any special cosseting.

The photographs of this lively breed, with its strong bones and abundant hair, were taken in Austria. The lively character of these charming horses shines through on all the pictures – whether they are portrait studies or action shots of a mare and her foal.

Fellow, the Welsh Cob stallion, trots cheerfully across a spring meadow.

With strength and courage he ventures forth. Movement is the greatest element of a horse.

Following pages: Portraits of the stallions Klon (left) and Fellow (right) at full gallop

Beautiful and intelligent – Lipizzaners

There are countless stories about the ancient and outstanding breed of Lipizzaner horses. The breed has brought forth classical riding horses that are outstanding for their eagerness to learn and ability to perform dressage tests of the highest possible standard.
The refined way in which these medium-sized, compact horses deport themselves is fascinating. They are muscular yet graceful. Arch-Duke Charles of Austria began breeding them in 1580 with thirty-three horses he imported from Spain. Subsequently the bloodlines of German horses were also introduced.
The breed gets its name from the stud at Lipica, where the horses lived until 1918, when they were moved to Piber.
Only those horses that showed an aptitude for dressage were used for breeding – rarely more than 150.
Although breeding was carried out with a small number of horses, degeneration of the breed was avoided by occasionally crossing-out to other bloodlines. By these means, it has been possible to maintain the high level of intelligence and agility for which the breed is renowned.
The best horses are still used in the Spanish Riding School in Vienna. The riders are all masters of the classical high school of riding.
The origins of the classical high school go back to the days of chivalry and the knights of old. Military equitation included exercises that still exist today as dressage tests. The cultural value that the riders uphold with their Lipizzaner stallions is incalculable.
The photographs, taken in Austria and at the stud in Lipica, resemble painted works of art.

A strong personality – the stallion Pluto Verona

A herd of Lipizzaners in the meadows at the Lipica stud: colts (left) and mares with foals (right).

The two Lipizzaner stallions embody a perfect symbiosis of strength and beauty

Playful duels between Fjord stallions

These photographs show Fjord stallions playfully fighting with each other. They were taken in Bavaria. Fjord ponies originate from the south-western coast of Norway and are distinguished by their light sallow or dun colouring with their eel-stripe and manes of partially black but also greyish-brown hair. The manes of those ponies living wild are usually thin but domesticated animals generally have their manes clipped so that they stand erect. These horses are kept as work-horses by Norwegian farmers, and used to haul timber. They are also frequently hitched between the shafts of a cart or trap. The stallions are still used in Norway to haul heavy wagons. Enthusiasts for the breed can get carried away when they describe the pony's gait: explaining the painstaking step, how they can maintain a trot for a long time, and about their powerful gallop. Other excellent characteristics of these fine ponies are their uncomplicated manner, their readiness to learn, and their alertness. These ponies are now widely used in Norway and elsewhere as friendly, sure-footed, docile riding ponies, as draught or pack-horses, or as attractive carriage horses.

The photographs depict the power of these horses with their primitive bodies as they playfully rear up, bite, and wrestle with their opponent with their front hooves.

These friendly duels are intended as a trial of strength for the young stallions.

Fjord pony stallions cautiously sniff each other.

The manes of these visitors from the wild consist of both black and greyish-brown hair. Their manes have been clipped according to fashion, making them stand erect.

Battle between rivals – drumming hooves and ferociously quick bites can lead to dangerous wounds.

Blows and bites are exchanged as they rear up.

A lull in the playful duel as they cautiously sniff each other.

Haflinger and Icelandic – lively ponies

The lively, nimble Haflingers are highly regarded as robust, small horses with strong, sound legs that are sure-footed.
This attractive mountain breed is predominantly long-haired chestnut with shades of almost white and other light hues.
The pictures taken in the Tyrol show a Haflinger stallion whickering, an atmospheric tableau of a herd in mist, and action studies of stallions.
The photographs reflect the boisterous, lively character of the breed that originates from a tough mountain horse from the Alps of South Tyrol. The Haflinger was created by cross-breeding with the coldblood Norik horses from the Alps and eastern horses that were brought back by the crusaders. Their appearance with sturdy legs and a wide range of uses has made them a recognized breed.
The Haflinger is the epitome of the symbolic friendly pony that steals everyone's heart.
The pleasure that both Haflingers and Icelandic ponies derive from gambolling in the snow is proved by the photographs on p128.

The herd of Icelandic ponies was photographed in Austria. The ponies are normally raised in a herd that lives outdoors the entire year. The merciless natural selection has resulted in one of the hardiest of breeds that can cope with almost anything.
Icelandic horses figure in Norse sagas and legends, such as that of Gráni, the horse of the Norse hero, Siegfried. The eyes of this intrepid small horse mirror the distant horizons, deep valleys, and ice-cold glaciers of their land of origin. In addition to walk, trot, and gallop, the Icelandic pony has two more gaits – pace, and tölt (a four-beat running walk). The texture of the coat and long hair on the quiff, mane, and tail, protect the pony from every type of weather.

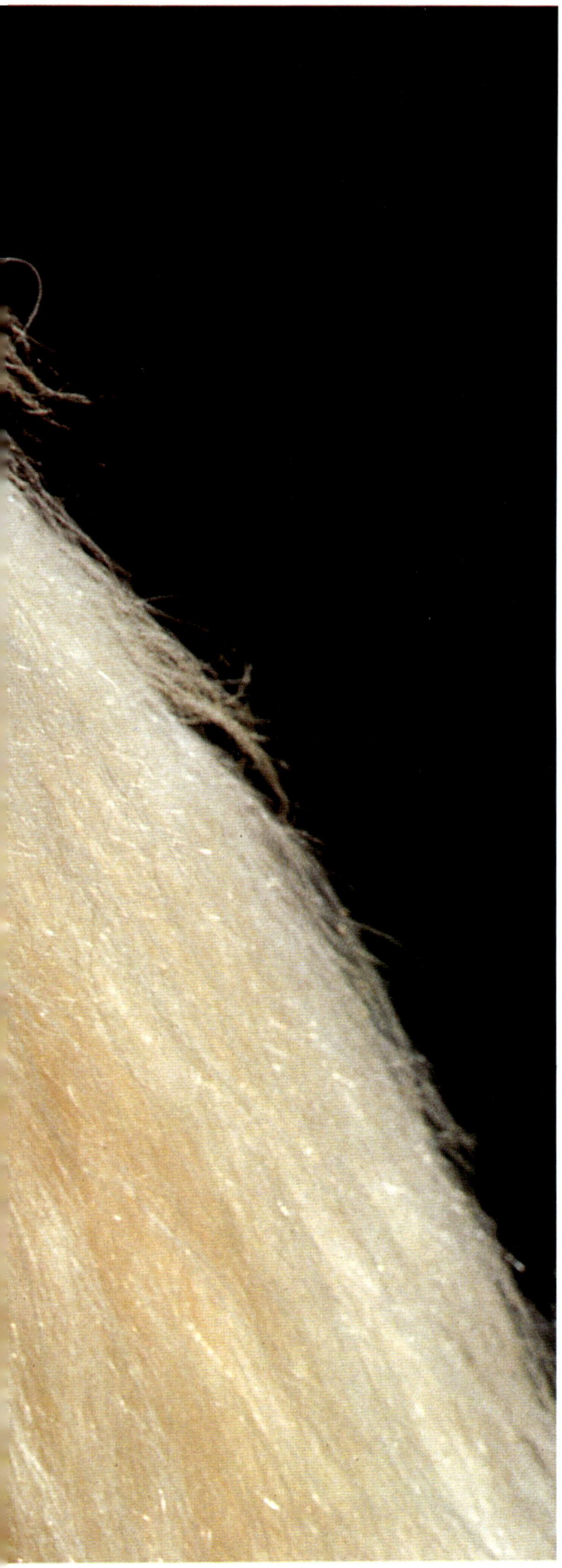

Portrait of a Haflinger stallion: a calm eye, flared nostrils, and dense mane that seems to be formed of strands of gold

Action studies of Haflinger stallions: the dance of the lively mountain ponies

Haflinger colts gambol in the snows of winter

The struggle for supremacy leads to powerful bites.

The horses' hooves kick up the snow to make an amazing image

Perfect beauty – Andalusian horses

During his travels through Europe to photograph horses, Tomás Mícek was drawn back once again to Andalusia.
This time he took a series of expressive photographs of Andalusian horses against backgrounds such as meadows carpeted with flowers.
The images document the fascination, intelligence, and good-nature of this Spanish breed.
Looking at these images can help you to share with him his enthusiasm for the Andalusian horse, and his love for these creatures.

"My horse is the dolphin of the prairie..."

Roy Campbell

"The world was mine until the day that he lifted his head and cried – but not because of me. The answer that he expected could only have been a whinny."

Robert Vavra

"A horse! A horse!
My Kingdom for a horse!"

William Shakespeare

"Much time must pass before ever
an Andalusian shall be born as
brave and as free as you;
I sing praises of your beauty
with plaintive words and
recall the wretched win in
the olive trees."

Frederico Carcia Lorca

The owners

ANDALUSIAN:
Miguel Angel Cárdenas Osuna, Ecija (Seville), Spain
Francisco Lazo Díaz, Hacienda Lerena, Carrion de los Céspedes, Spain
The Terry Stud, General Mola 2, Puerta de Santa Maria, Spain

ARABS:
Christian and Rachel Bourrasse, Harras de Nautiac, Tosse, France
Mariangeles Delclaux, Manás de la Hoz, Centro ecuestre, Liendo, Spain
Dr. W. Georg Olms, Hamasa Stud, Treis/Lda., Hesse, Germany
Miguel Osuna Saavedra, Cortijo Cassas Alba, Ecija (Seville), Spain
Josef and Regina Pirklbauer, Grösslinggut, Freistadt, Austria
Richard and Brigitte Roques, Domaines de Ninaute, Limoux, France
Jean-Marc and Christine Valerio, Haras d'Ainhoa, La Vielle Einseigne, Hasparen, France
Bertrand and Christine Valette, Mas de Lafon, Le Segur, Monesties, France

THOROUGHBREDS:
Napajedla Stud, Zamecka 582, Southern Moravia, Czech Republic

FRIESIAN HORSES:
Cor and Martina de Jong, Friesen Trainings-Center Federath, Overath, Germany
Bernd and Marie-Claire Reisgies, Gut Amtmannscherf, Odenthal, Germany

LIPIZZANERS:
Balthasar Alois Hauser, 'Stanglwirt', Going am Wilden Kaiser, Tyrol, Austria
Lipizzaner Stud Lipica, Sezana, Slovenia.

WELSH COBS:
Milos Welde, Gschwendthof, Maria Anzbach, Austria

CAMARGUE HORSES:
Gilbert Arnaud, Mas De L'Eveillat, Les Saintes-Maries de la Mer, Camargue, France
Françoise and André Peytavin, Manade Salierene, Saliers, Camargue, France

FJORD PONIES:
Barbara Schacker and Christina Tietgen, Ponyreithof, St. Margarethen, Branneburg, Bavaria, Germany

HAFLINGERS:
Haflinger Pferdezuchtverband Tirol, Fohlenhof, Austria

ICELANDIC PONIES:
Josef and Ingeborg Mayr, Sporthotel Parcours, Ampflwang, Austria
Barbara Schacker, Ponyreithof, St. Margarethen, Branneburg, Bavaria, Germany

Acknowledgements

Many people have made my work on this book easier with their tremendous help and friendship. I wish to thank them all heartily.

My special thanks in Spain go to: Miguel Angel Cárdenas Osuna and Miguel Enrile Osuna, and also to their head of stables Antonio Calvo Aguilera; the estate manager of the Finca El Corrin, Rafael Rodríguez Martín; Fernando Gago García, press manager of the Terry Stud; Francisco Lazo Díaz and his estate manager Sánches Carrasco; Miguel Osuna Saavedra, Antonio Diosdado Galán, Diego Diez Domecq, Fernando Escalera de la Escalera, Manuel de Novales Vasco, commandant of the Vicos military stud; Luis Ybara and their manager Rafael Romero Complido and his son Rafael Romero Ramos; Ulrike Marcik van de Finca for Shagya Arabs 'La Canada del Robledo'; Marieangeles Delcalux, Eduardo Via Dufresne, and Roland Kreher. I was given valuable advice by Kristian Fenaux and I wish to thank my Parisian friend Felix Ktorza, expert on Andalusian horses, for the rapidity with which he arranged certain photo-sessions in Spain.

In France, Christel Siebert prepared the ground for my photographic visits to many owners and opened the way for me. All the French owners whose horses I photographed co-operated with great interest and contributed to the outcome: Gilbert Arnaud, Rachel and Christian Bourrasse, Max Dardenne, Marc Jalabert, Jean-Luc Jardel, Françoise and André Peytavin, Cécile and Richard Philström, Brigitte and Richard Roques, Christine and Jean-Marc Valerio, Christine and Bertrand Valette.

In Germany, I was able to photograph the lovely Asil Arabs of W. Georg Olms several times. Barbara Schacker, Christina Tietgen and the entire team of horse-lovers at the stables in St. Margarethen have often helped me enormously. I am much indebted also to Marie-Claire and Bernd Resigies, Martina and Cor de Jong, and also Christa and Hans-Joachim Dannesfelser. They all own wonderful Friesian horses and I have had much support in my work from them.

In Austria, I wish to give my warmest thanks to: Josef and Ingeborg Mayr of the Ampflwang Icelandic Stud; Johannes Schweisgut, Robert Mair, and Gerhard Blasnik of the Tyrolean Haflinger foal nursery in Ebbs. Milos Welde let me take photographs of his superb Welsh Cobs and Baltasar Alois Hauser permitted me to photograph his priceless Lipizzaner stallion. I also owe much gratitude to Regina and Josef Pirklbauer.

In Slovenia, my thanks are directed to Andrej Franetic and Vili Borjancic for making it possible for me to photograph their valuable and attractive stallions at Lipica.

I wish also to thank my Czech friends Zdenek Hlacik, Dr. Antonín Cernotsky, Jan Sádlo, and all other friends who helped me with the photography, not forgetting the people at the Napajedla Thoroughbred Stud in Southern Moravia.

Liebenau, May 1995

Tomás Mícek